Raptor World

Condors

by Jenna Lee Gleisner

Bullfrog Books

Ideas for Parents and Teachers

Bullfrog Books let children practice reading informational text at the earliest reading levels. Repetition, familiar words, and photo labels support early readers.

Before Reading
- Discuss the cover photo. What does it tell them?
- Look at the picture glossary together. Read and discuss the words.

Read the Book
- "Walk" through the book and look at the photos. Let the child ask questions. Point out the photo labels.
- Read the book to the child, or have him or her read independently.

After Reading
- Prompt the child to think more. Ask: Condors are scavengers that eat dead animals. Do you know of any other animals that are scavengers?

Bullfrog Books are published by Jump!
5357 Penn Avenue South
Minneapolis, MN 55419
www.jumplibrary.com

Library of Congress Cataloging-in-Publication Data

Names: Gleisner, Jenna Lee, author.
Title: Condors / by Jenna Lee Gleisner.
Description: Bullfrog books edition.
Minneapolis, MN : Jump!, Inc., [2020]
Series: Raptor World
Audience: Age 5-8. | Audience: K to Grade 3.
Includes index.
Identifiers: LCCN 2018040688 (print)
LCCN 2018041701 (ebook)
ISBN 9781641286374 (ebook)
ISBN 9781641286367 (hardcover : alk. paper)
ISBN 9781641288194 (pbk.)
Subjects: LCSH: Condors—Juvenile literature.
Classification: LCC QL696.C53 (ebook)
LCC QL696.C53 G54 2020 (print)
DDC 598.9/2—dc23
LC record available at https://lccn.loc.gov/2018040688

Editor: Susanne Bushman
Designer: Jenna Casura

Photo Credits: George Lamson/Shutterstock, cover; aaltair/Shutterstock, 1; Iakov Filimonov/Shutterstock, 3; Arthur Dressler/age fotostock/SuperStock, 4, 23br; Cyril Ruoso/Minden Pictures/SuperStock, 5; Oscar Espinosa/Alamy, 6-7; Don Mammoser/Shutterstock, 8-9, 23tm; Kurt Moses/National Park Service, 10-11; JPLDesigns/iStock, 12-13, 23bm; wrangel/iStock, 14, 23tl; photoshooter2015/Shutterstock, 15; Steve Johnson/Getty, 16-17, 23tr; Murray Cooper/Minden Pictures/Age Fotostock, 18; Leeloona, 19; TUI DE ROY/Minden Pictures/Age Fotostock, 20-21; Martin Mecnarowski/Shutterstock, 22; Ad_hominem/Shutterstock, 23bl; Eric Isselee/Shutterstock, 24.

Printed in the United States of America at Corporate Graphics in North Mankato, Minnesota.

Table of Contents

Bald Birds

A bald condor soars.

It is up high.

Why?

To look for food.

It can see well.

These birds fly far.

Their wings are big.

And long!

Up to 10 feet
(3 meters) across!

collar

There are two kinds.
The Andean condor
is one.

See its white collar?

The California condor
is the other.

It is the largest flying bird!

Where?

In North America.

Wow!

They are scavengers.

Look! A dead animal to eat.

Yum!

They have sharp beaks.

beak

Why?

To tear food.

It will feed its baby.

It saves some food.

Where?

In its crop.

crop

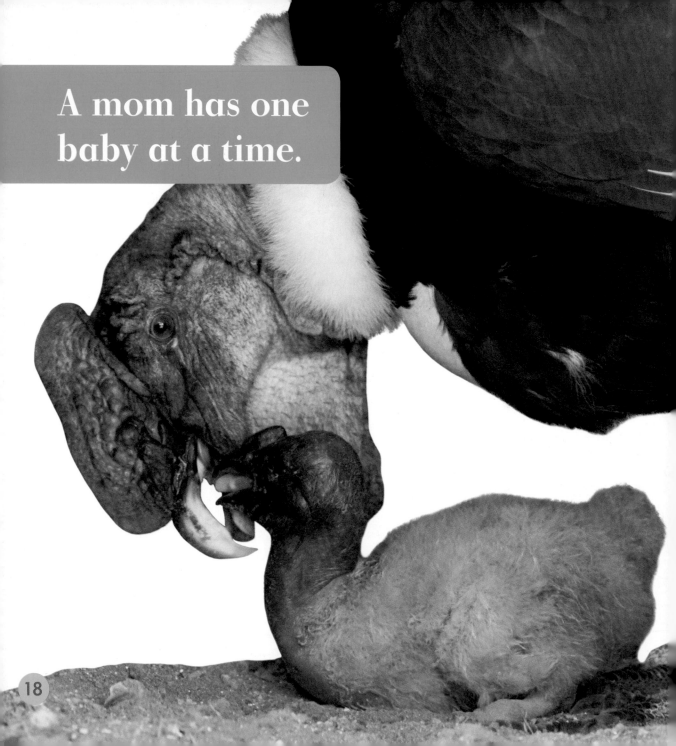

A mom has one baby at a time.

It grows up in a cave.

The baby grows.

It learns.

It will find food.

young
condor

Built to Soar

head
Condors have bald heads with no feathers. This keeps them from getting too messy while they eat.

wings
Huge wings help a condor soar and stay in the air for hours.

beak
The beak is curved and sharp to help the condor tear its food.

crop
Parents store and carry food in their crops. They regurgitate it to feed their baby chick until the baby learns to find food for itself.

Picture Glossary

bald
Having little or no hair on the head.

collar
A band or strip around the neck.

crop
The pouch in a bird's throat where food is stored.

North America
The continent made of the United States, Canada, Mexico, and Central America.

scavengers
Animals that feed on dead or decaying animals.

soars
Flies or glides high in the air.

Index

To Learn More

Finding more information is as easy as 1, 2, 3.

❶ Go to www.factsurfer.com

❷ Enter "condors" into the search box.

❸ Click the "Surf" button to see a list of websites.